CW01316719

COOKING FOR PROGRAMMERS
0x00 - SIMPLE RECIPES ON THE CMD

A cookbook for programmers could have a variety of features that are specifically tailored to the needs and interests of programmers.

Quick and easy recipes that can be made with minimal prep time, since programmers often have busy schedules and may not have a lot of time to spend in the kitchen.

Recipes that can be made with common pantry staples, since programmers may not always have access to a fully stocked kitchen.

Recipes that can be made in bulk and frozen or stored in the fridge for later, so that programmers can have ready-made meals on hand when they're short on time.

Recipes that can be made using minimal kitchen equipment, such as a single pot or a microwave, since programmers may not always have access to a full kitchen.

Tips and tricks for making healthy meals that are easy to transport, since programmers may need to eat at their desks or on the go.

Ideas for programming-themed meals, such as dishes inspired by different programming languages or dishes that are served at software development conferences.

Recipe notes and tips for adapting recipes for different dietary restrictions, such as gluten-free or vegetarian diets.

Overall, a cookbook for programmers could be a great resource for anyone who wants to eat well and stay healthy while working in the tech industry.

This book does not include any of these features, it is just meant to be fun!

Richard

COOKING FOR PROGRAMMERS 0x00

TABLE OF CONTENTS

If you're a programmer, you know that coding can be an incredibly rewarding and satisfying activity.

But have you ever thought about combining your love of programming with your love of cooking? By bringing the two together?

Whether you're cooking for your family or just for yourself, the recipes are designed to be flexible and adaptable to your needs. I know how busy life can be, and I want to make it easier for you to eat well and enjoy home-cooked meals, even on busy weeknights.

4
Oven Vegetables

Oven roasted vegetables tend to be very flavorful, as the high heat of the oven caramelizes the natural sugars in the vegetables, which intensifies their flavor.

6
Pizza Toast

The versatility of being able to customize the toppings to suit your own preferences, whether you like a classic margherita pizza or something more adventurous.

8
Rice Pudding

The creamy, rich texture of the pudding. The nostalgia factor of rice pudding, which is often associated with childhood memories and comfort food.

10
Simple Carbonara

A simple version without eggs. The combination of the noodles with the rich, flavorful and simple sauce creates a satisfying and tasty dish.

12
Espresso

Rich, creamy texture: The high pressure used to extract espresso creates a creamy, velvety texture that many people find particularly enjoyable.

14
Tomato Coconut Soup

The smooth and velvety soup is both comforting and satisfying, with the addition of spices and seasonings adding depth and complexity to the flavor.

COOKING FOR PROGRAMMERS 0x00

16 — MATLAB®
Millet with Vegetables

A tasty and nutritious meal with nutty millet and flavorful vegetables, rich in vitamins and minerals.

17
Crepes

Or "Palatschinken". The thin, tender texture of crepes allows them to be easily filled with a variety of sweet or savory fillings.

18 — C#
Curd Cake

This one-bowl version cheesecake is easy to make with minimal dishwashing. Note: not for weight-watching. :-)

22 — Rust
Turkey in the Oven

Turkey is a lean protein source that is rich in nutrients such as vitamin B6. You can use different types of cheese or add different herbs or spices to change up the flavor.

23 — GO
Rice Vegetable Casserole

It can be served as a side dish or main course, depending on your preferences and the portion size. It can also be easily customized to suit different dietary needs or preferences.

25 — JAVA
Carrot Cake

One of the things that makes carrot cake special is the combination of sweet and savory ingredients which creates a unique flavor profile.

COOKING FOR PROGRAMMERS 0x00

28   Perl 5

Spicy Meat Strudel

Spicy Meat Strudel is a puff pastry filled with a sautéed meat and vegetable mixture, layered with cream cheese, and baked until golden.

32

Emperor's Mess

Kaiserschmarrn, often translated as "Emperor's Mess" or "Emperor's Shred", is a popular traditional dessert from Austria.

36

Creamy Ham Spätzle

The salty and smoky taste of the ham pairs well with the creamy and tangy sour cream. The recipe is quite flexible.

38   Ada

South Tyrolean Apple Strudel

South Tyrol, a region in Northern Italy - Buttery and crumbly texture - a cultural experience.

42   [+.]

???

Its structure provides a wealth of possibilities in terms of both preparation and flavor. One of the most versatile ingredients in the kitchen.

COOKING FOR PROGRAMMERS 0x00

OVEN VEGETABLES
JAVASCRIPT

```javascript
class OvenVegetableRecipe {
  constructor() {
    this.name = "Oven Vegetables";
    this.servings = 4;
    this.ingredients = [
      {
        name: "small potatoes",
        quantity: 500,
        unit: "g"
      },
      {
        name: "peppers",
        quantity: 300,
        unit: "g"
      },
      {
        name: "shallots",
        quantity: 4
      },
      {
        name: "bundle of fresh Italian herbs",
        quantity: 1,
        // Optional
        herbs: ["thyme", "oregano", "marjoram", "rosemary"]
      },
      {
        name: "cherry tomatoes",
        quantity: 200,
        unit: "g"
      },
      {
        name: "mushrooms",
        quantity: 150,
        unit: "g"
      },
      {
        name: "garlic cloves",
        quantity: 6-8
      },
      {
        name: "olive oil",
        quantity: 4,
        unit: "tablespoons"
      },
```

COOKING FOR PROGRAMMERS 0x00

```js
      {
        name: "sea salt"
      },
      {
        name: "black pepper"
      },
      {
        name: "paprika powder",
        quantity: 1,
        unit: "teaspoon"
      }
    ];
    this.instructions = [
      'Preheat the oven to 200°C (fan oven 180°C).',
      'Wash the potatoes, brush them and halve them lengthwise. Wash the peppers, clean them and cut \
      them into large pieces. Peel the shallots and quarter or eight them depending on their size.',
      'Wash the herbs, shake them dry, optionally pluck the leaves and chop them or leave the herbs whole',
      'Wash the tomatoes, clean the mushrooms, peel the garlic and halve everything.',
      'Heat the oil in a large frying pan and fry the potatoes in it for 3-4 minutes. Add the peppers \
      and shallots and fry briefly.',
      'Add the tomatoes, mushrooms and garlic and mix well. Season the vegetables with sea salt, pepper \
      and paprika powder and mix in the herbs.',
      'Spread the vegetables and the complete oil from the frying pan evenly on a baking sheet and bake \
      in the hot oven (middle) for 25-30 minutes.',
    ];
  }

  printIngredients = () => {
    console.log(`Ingredients for ${this.servings} servings of ${this.name}:`);
    this.ingredients.forEach(ingredient => {
      console.log(
        `- ${ingredient.quantity??''}${ingredient.unit ?? ''}${
          ingredient.unit || ingredient.quantity ? ' ' : ''
        }${ingredient.name}`,
      );
    });
  }

  printInstructions = () => {
    console.log(`\n\nInstructions for ${this.name}:`);
    this.instructions.forEach((instruction, index) => {
      console.log(`${index + 1}. ${instruction}\n`);
    });
  };

}
let ov = new OvenVegetableRecipe();
ov.printIngredients();
ov.printInstructions();
```

PIZZA TOAST
C++

```cpp
#include <iostream>
#include <string>

const std::string ingredients[10] = {
"toast slices", "sour cream", "corn",
"peppers","ham", "grated cheese",
"spring onions","salt", "pepper",
"pizza spice"
};

int main() {
    int oven_temperature = 180;
    std::cout << "Preheating oven to " << oven_temperature << "°C.";
    std::cout << "Distributing ingredients(";
    int size = sizeof(ingredients) / sizeof(ingredients[0]);
    for(int i = 1; i < size; i++)
    {
        std::cout << ingredients[i];
        if(i < size-1)
         std::cout << ", ";
    }
    std::cout << ") on toast slices." << std::endl;
    int baking_time = 20;
    std::cout << "Baking in preheated oven for about ";
    std::cout << baking_time << " minutes until golden brown." << std::endl;
    std::cout << "Pizza toast is ready!" << std::endl;
    return 0;
}
```

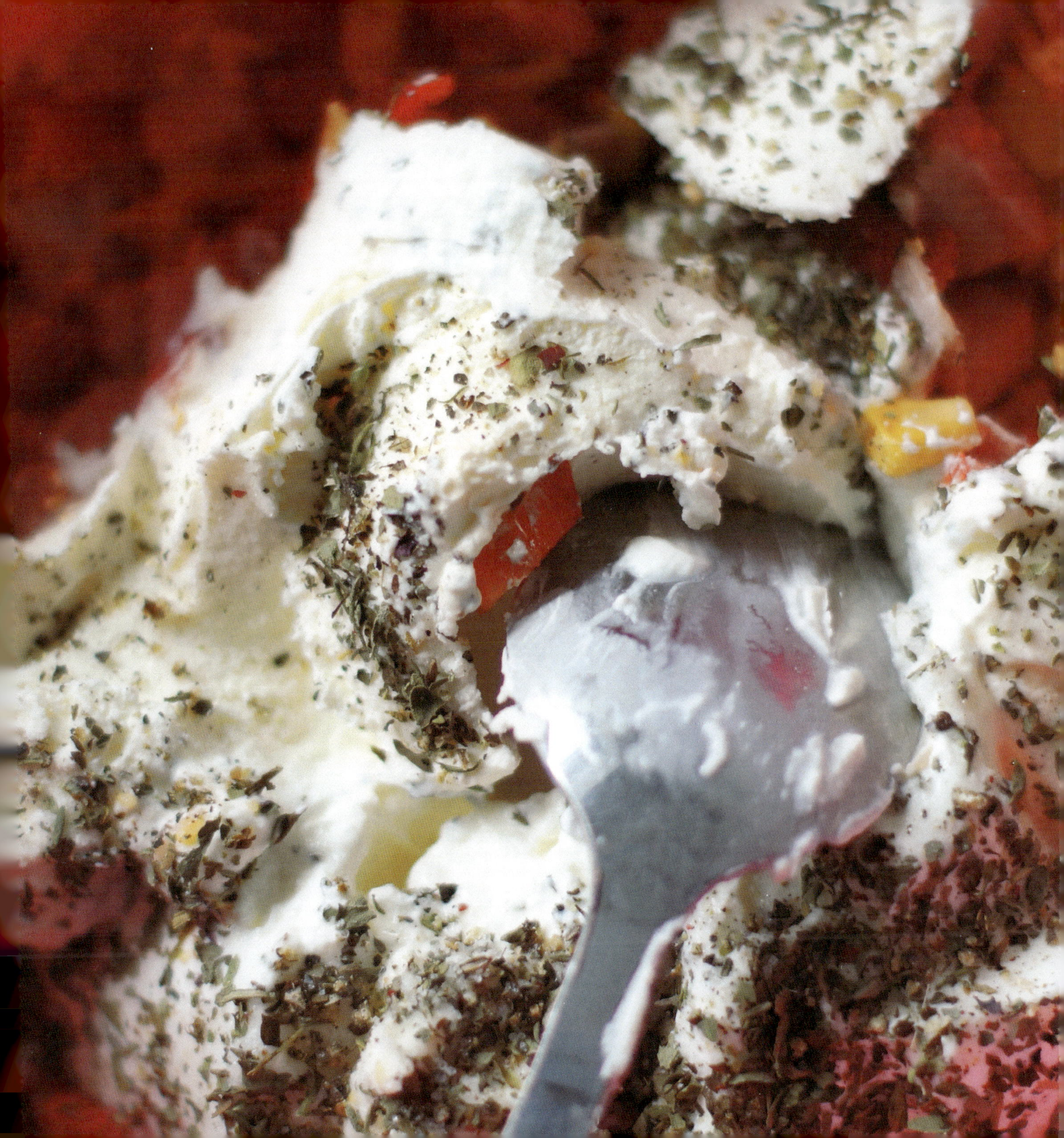

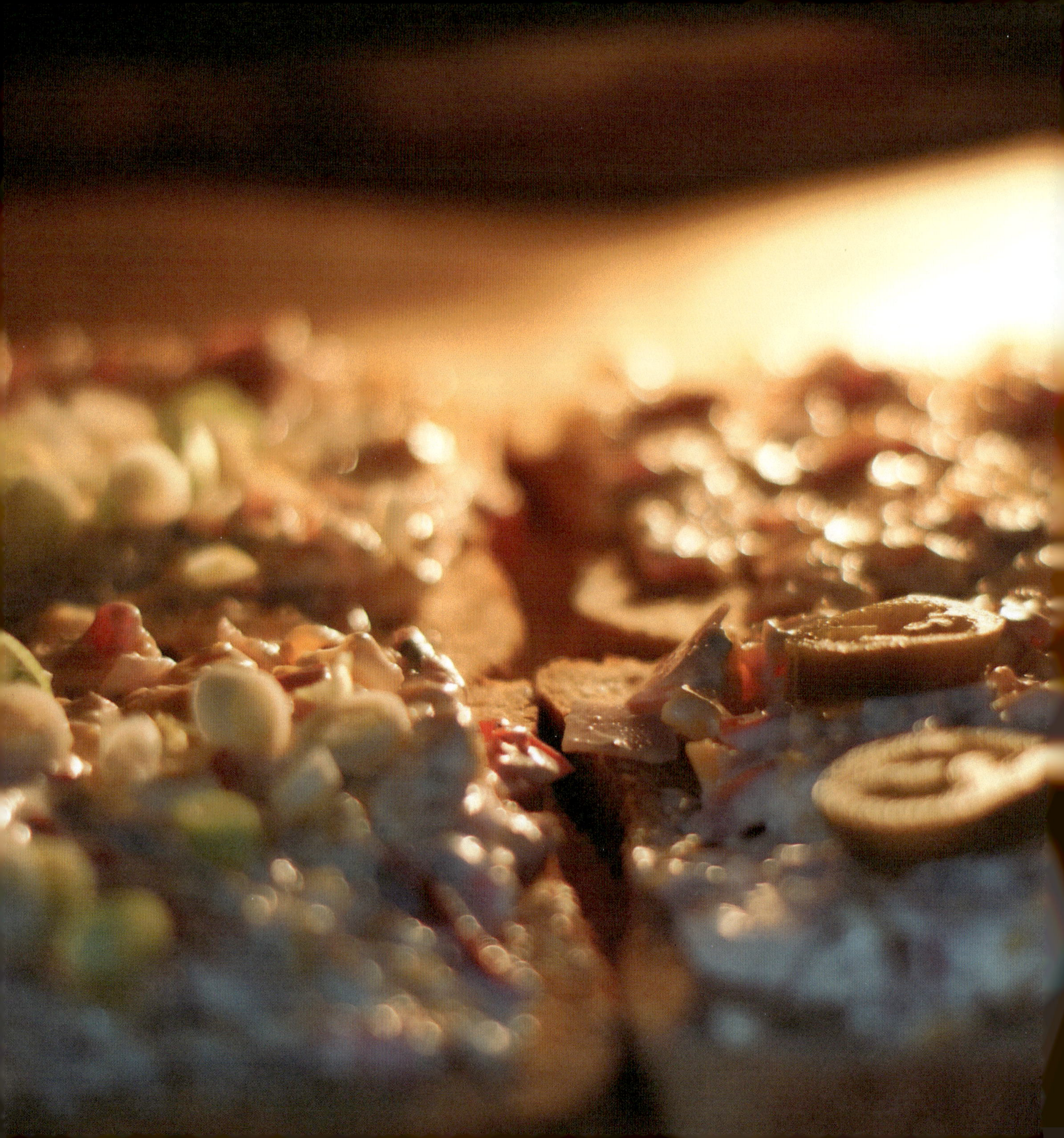

RICE PUDDING
PHP

```php
<?php

$ingredients = [
    "600ml milk",
    "125g risotto rice",
    "2 tablespoons sugar",
    "1 package vanilla sugar",
    "1 pinch salt"
];

function boilMilk($milk, $sugar, $salt) {
    echo "Bring milk, sugar, and salt to boil.\n";
}

function addRice($rice) {
    echo "Add risotto rice.\n";
}

function simmerRice() {
    echo "Lett rice simmer for 30 minutes, stirr occasionally.\n";
}

function cookRicePudding() {
    global $ingredients;
    [$milk, $rice, $sugar, $vanilla, $salt] = $ingredients;
    boilMilk($milk, $sugar, $salt);
    addRice($rice);
    simmerRice();
    echo "Rice pudding is ready!\n";
}

cookRicePudding();
?>
```

The sweet, comforting flavor of the pudding, which is enhanced by the addition of sugar and spices like cinnamon and vanilla.

The versatility of the pudding, which can be served hot or cold, and can be topped with a variety of toppings like fruit, nuts, or chocolate chips.

The creamy, rich texture of the pudding, which is made by slowly cooking the rice in milk until it is soft and tender.

Overall, rice pudding is a delicious and satisfying dessert that is perfect for satisfying a sweet tooth or for enjoying as a comfort food.

"Not only for children, also perfect for programmers!"

COOKING FOR PROGRAMMERS 0x00

SIMPLE CARBONARA
TYPESCRIPT

```typescript
type IngredientUnit =
  | 'kg'
  | 'g'
  | 'ml'
  | 'l'
  | 'tsp'
  | 'tbsp'
  | 'pinch'
  | 'handful'
  | 'piece'
  ;

interface Ingredient {
  name: string;
  amount: number;
  iunit: IngredientUnit;
}

type Instruction = string;

interface Recipe {
  name: string;
  ingredients: Ingredient[];
  instructions: Instruction[];
}

const carbonara: Recipe = {
  name: 'Light Carbonara Sauce',
  ingredients: [
    { name: 'Pasta', amount: 0.5, iunit: 'kg' },
    { name: 'Ham', amount: 100, iunit: 'g' },
    { name: 'Onion', amount: 1, iunit: 'piece' },
    { name: 'Garlic clove', amount: 1, iunit: 'piece' },
    { name: 'Milk', amount: 200, iunit: 'ml' },
    { name: 'Flour', amount: 1, iunit: 'tbsp' },
    { name: 'Salt', amount: 1, iunit: 'pinch' },
    { name: 'Pepper', amount: 1, iunit: 'pinch' },
    { name: 'Parsley', amount: 1, iunit: 'handful' },
  ],
  instructions: [
    'Fry the onion and add the garlic.',
    'Sprinkle flour over the mixture and pour in the milk.',
    'Boil briefly until a creamy sauce is formed.',
    'Add the ham and season with salt and pepper.',
    'Add pasta as desired and serve with fresh parsley.',
  ],
};
```

```typescript
function printRecipe(recipe: Recipe) {
  console.log(recipe.name);
  console.log('Ingredients:');
  recipe.ingredients.forEach((ingredient) => {
    console.log(
      `- ${ingredient.amount} ${getUnitString(ingredient.iunit)} ${
        ingredient.name
      }`,
    );
  });
  console.log('Instructions:');
  recipe.instructions.forEach((instruction, index) => {
    console.log(`${index + 1}. ${instruction}`);
  });
}

function getUnitString(iunit: IngredientUnit) {
  switch (iunit) {
    case 'kg':
      return 'kg';
    case 'g':
      return 'g';
    case 'ml':
      return 'ml';
    case 'l':
      return 'l';
    case 'tsp':
      return 'tsp';
    case 'tbsp':
      return 'tbsp';
    case 'pinch':
      return 'pinch';
    case 'handful':
      return 'handful';
    case 'piece':
      return 'piece';
    default:
      return '';
  }
}

printRecipe(carbonara);
```

COOKING FOR PROGRAMMERS 0x00

ESPRESSO
PYTHON

```python
import time

class EspressoMachine:
    def __init__(self):
        self.current_temperature = 0
        self.current_amount_brewed = 0

    def heat_water(self, temperature):
        # simulate heating up the water
        time.sleep(1)
        self.current_temperature = temperature

    def insert_portafilter(self, portafilter):
        # simulate inserting the portafilter into the machine
        time.sleep(0.5)

    def start_brewing(self):
        # simulate starting the brewing process
        time.sleep(1)
        self.current_amount_brewed = 0

    def stop_brewing(self):
        # simulate stopping the brewing process
        time.sleep(0.5)

    def current_brewed(self):
        # simulate the current amount of espresso brewed
        self.current_amount_brewed += 0.5
        return self.current_amount_brewed

class Portafilter:
    def fill(self, ground_beans):
        # simulate filling the portafilter with ground beans
        time.sleep(0.5)

class Tamper:
    def tamp(self, portafilter):
        # simulate using the tamper to compress the grounds
        time.sleep(0.5)
```

```python
class CoffeeCup:
    def serve(self):
        # simulate serving the coffee
        return "Enjoy your delicious portafilter coffee!"

def prepare_coffee(espresso_machine, portafilter, ground_beans, tamper, water, desired_amount):
    # Fill the portafilter with ground espresso beans and tamp down lightly
    portafilter.fill(ground_beans)
    tamper.tamp(portafilter)

    # Place the portafilter in the espresso machine and lock it in place
    espresso_machine.insert_portafilter(portafilter)

    # Heat up the water in the espresso machine until it reaches the desired temperature
    espresso_machine.heat_water(200)

    # Place a coffee cup under the portafilter and begin the espresso brewing process
    coffee_cup = CoffeeCup()
    espresso_machine.start_brewing()

    # As the espresso is brewed, it will flow into the cup. When the desired amount has been
    # brewed, stop the process.
    while espresso_machine.current_brewed() < desired_amount:
        time.sleep(0.5)
    espresso_machine.stop_brewing()

    # Serve the espresso immediately
    return coffee_cup.serve()

espresso_machine = EspressoMachine()
portafilter = Portafilter()
tamper = Tamper()
ground_beans = "Espresso beans"
water = "Water"
desired_amount = 1.5

print(prepare_coffee(espresso_machine, portafilter, ground_beans, tamper, water, desired_amount))
```

COOKING FOR PROGRAMMERS 0x00

TOMATO COCONUT SOUP
R

The combination of tomatoes and coconut milk creates a creamy, smooth texture that is satisfying to eat.

Tomatoes are naturally sweet and acidic, which adds depth and balance to the flavor of the soup.

Coconut milk is a rich and flavorful ingredient that adds a tropical twist to the soup.

The combination of spices and herbs used in the recipe can also contribute to the overall deliciousness of the soup.

```r
ingredients <- list(
    list(name = "Tomato puree", amount = 500, unit = "ml"),
    list(name = "Coconut milk", amount = 400, unit = "ml"),
    list(name = "Vegetable broth", amount = 250, unit = "ml"),
    list(name = "Spring onion", amount = 1, unit = "bundle"),
    list(name = "Oil", amount = 1, unit = "tbsp"),
    list(name = "Lemon juice", amount = 1, unit = "tbsp"),
    list(name = "Salt", amount = 1, unit = "pinch"),
    list(name = "Pepper", amount = 1, unit = "pinch"),
    list(name = "Sugar", amount = 1, unit = "pinch")
)

instructions <- c(
    "Cut the spring onion into rings and fry in oil.",
    "Add the tomato puree, vegetable broth, and coconut milk.",
    "Simmer over low heat for about ten minutes.",
    "Season with salt, pepper, sugar, and lemon juice."
)
```

COOKING FOR PROGRAMMERS 0x00

```r
print_recipe <- function(name, ingredients, instructions) {
  cat(name, "\n")
  cat("Ingredients:\n")
  for (ingredient in ingredients) {
    cat(sprintf("- %d %s %s\n", ingredient$amount, ingredient$unit, ingredient$name))
  }
  cat("Instructions:\n")
  for (i in seq_along(instructions)) {
    cat(sprintf("%d. %s\n", i, instructions[i]))
  }
}

print_recipe("Creamy Tomato Soup with Coconut", ingredients, instructions)
```

MILLET WITH VEGETABLES
MATLAB®

```matlab
function main()
    str_array = string(["40","Spring onions, carrots, zucchini, peppers", ...
        "feta cheese"]);
    amount_of_millet = str2double(str_array(1));
    vegetables = str_array(2);
    cheese = str_array(3);
    millet_amount = str2double("1");
    water_amount = str2double("2");
    millet_help = "Bring to a boil, then reduce to a simmer, cover" + ...
        ", " + "and cook for 18-20 minutes or until liquid is absorbed";
    fprintf("Cooking %dg of millet with %dg of water (%s).\n", ...
        millet_amount * amount_of_millet, water_amount * ...
        amount_of_millet, millet_help);
    fprintf("Frying %s...\n", vegetables);
    fprintf("Adding spices and %s...\n", cheese);
    % Create a circulant matrix of size 11-by-11.
    % A circulant matrix is a special kind of Toeplitz matrix
    % Why? Because it is MATLAB ;-)
    A = gallery('circul',11);
    imagesc(A);
end
```

COOKING FOR PROGRAMMERS 0x00

CREPES
RUBY

```ruby
def main
  # Parse command line arguments
  if ARGV.length != 1
    raise "Expected 1 argument: pieces
    of crepes to make"
  end
  pieces = ARGV[0].to_i

  # Mix ingredients
  flour = 25 * pieces
  eggs = 0.2 * pieces
  milk = 0.05 * pieces
  oil = 1
  sugar = 0.1 * pieces
  puts "Mixing #{flour}g of flour,
  #{eggs} eggs, #{milk}l of milk,
  #{oil} tablespoon of oil, and
  #{sugar} tablespoon of sugar..."

  # Fry the crepes
  puts "Frying crepes..."
  pieces.times do
    puts "Flipping crepe..."
  end

  puts "Done!"
end

main


$ ruby crepes.rb 10
```

CURD CAKE
C#

```csharp
using System;
using System.Linq;

namespace NoBottomCheesecake
{
    class Program
    {
        static void Main(string[] args)
        {
            var cheesecake = new Cheesecake();
            Console.WriteLine("Would you like to add raisins to your cheesecake (y/n)?");
            string addRaisins = Console.ReadLine();
            if (addRaisins.ToLower() == "y")
            {
                Console.WriteLine("How many tablespoons of raisins would you like to add?");
                string raisinInput = Console.ReadLine();
                double raisinAmount = double.Parse(raisinInput);
                cheesecake.AddRaisins(raisinAmount);
            }
            Console.WriteLine("Preheating oven to 180 degrees Celsius (350 degrees Fahrenheit)...");
            Console.WriteLine("Greasing springform pan with butter...");
            cheesecake.Bake();
            Console.ReadKey();
        }
    }
}
```

```csharp
class Cheesecake
{
    private const double ButterAmount = 250;
    private const double SugarAmount = 190;
    private const int EggAmount = 4;
    private const int CheesecakeAmount = 1000;
    // optional ingredients
    private bool UseRaisins { get; set; }
    private double RaisinAmount { get; set; }

    public Cheesecake()
    {
        UseRaisins = false;
        RaisinAmount = 0;
    }

    public void AddRaisins(double raisinAmount)
    {
        UseRaisins = true;
        RaisinAmount = raisinAmount;
    }

    public void Bake()
    {
        Console.WriteLine("Creaming together butter and sugar in mixing bowl...");
        Console.WriteLine("Adding eggs and mixing...");
        Console.WriteLine("Adding cheesecake and optional raisins and mixing...");
        if (UseRaisins)
        {
            Console.WriteLine($"Adding {RaisinAmount} tablespoons of raisins...");
        }
        Console.WriteLine("Baking for 45 minutes...");
    }
}
```

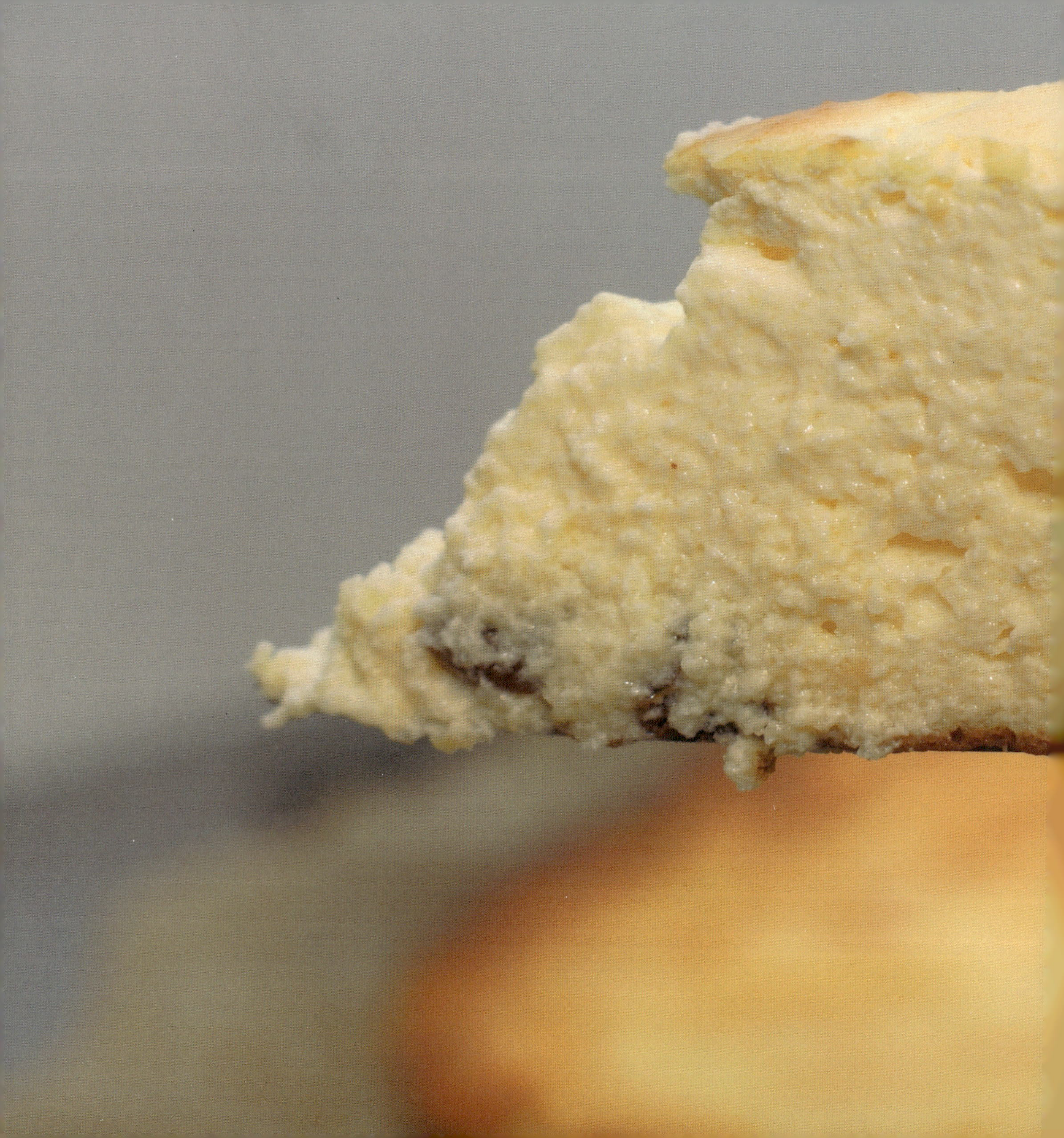

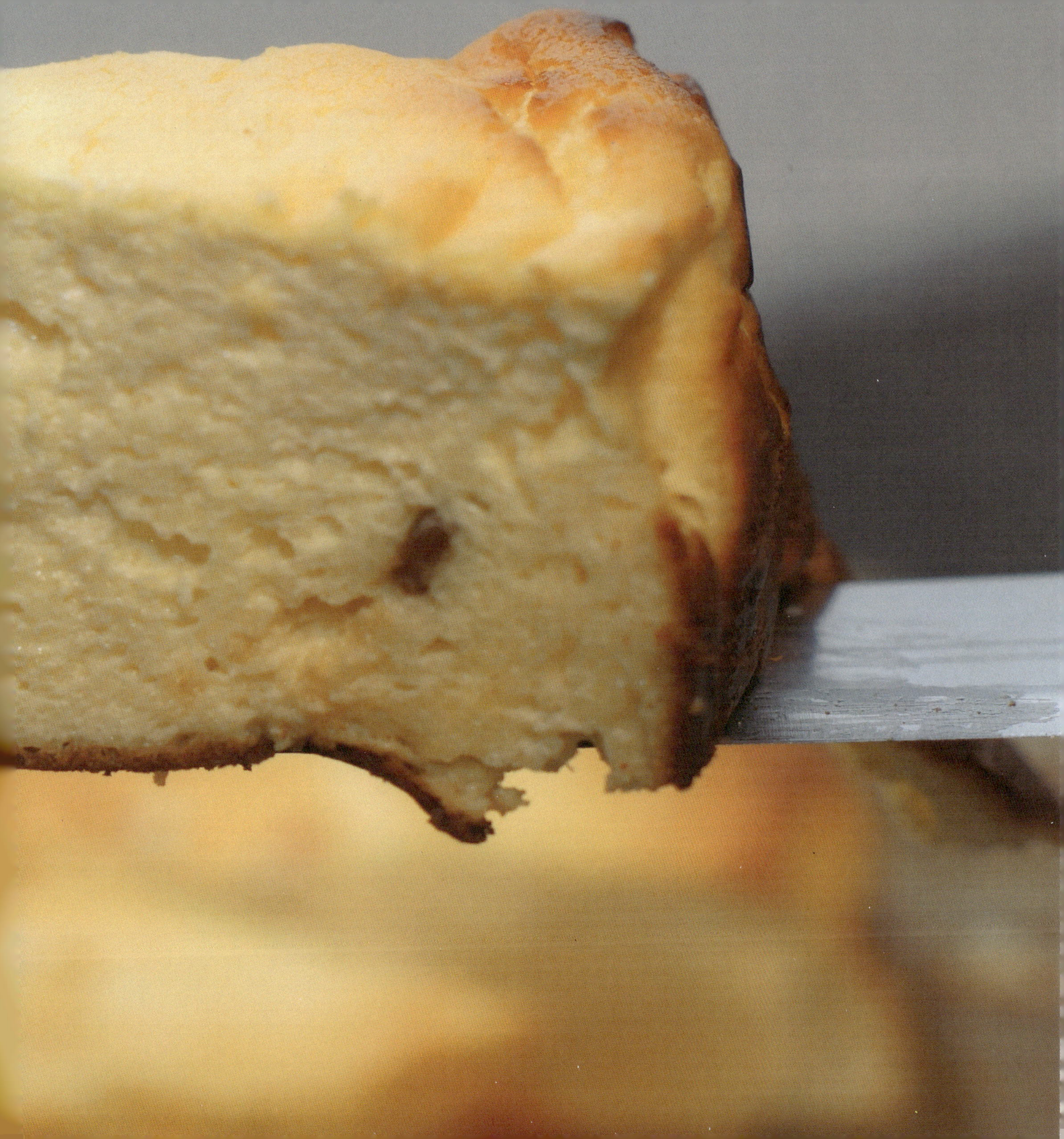

COOKING FOR PROGRAMMERS 0x00

TURKEY IN THE OVEN
RUST

```rust
fn main() {
    let ingredients = [
        ("Dice", 125, "g Mozzarella"),
        ("Grate", 15, "g Parmesan"),
        ("Chop", 10, " dried tomatoes"),
        ("Chop", 2, " garlic cloves"),
        ("Roughly chop", 5, "basil leaves"),
        ("Cut", 500, "g turkey breast fillet in 5cm pieces"),
        ("Season", 500,"g turkey breast fillet with salt"),
        ("Heat", 1, " tablespoon oil or butter"),
        ("Fry", 500,"g turkey breast fillet"),
        ("Season", 500,"g turkey breast fillet with pepper"),
        ("Add", 250, "g cream"),
        ("Stir and melt", 50, "g herb cream cheese"),
    ];

    // Prepare the ingredients.
    for (operation, value, ingredient) in ingredients.iter() {
        let prepared_ingredient = prepare(&operation.to_string(), *value, &ingredient.to_string());
        println!("{}", prepared_ingredient);
    }
    println!("{}",preheat_oven(200, 180));
    println!("{}",bake(25));
}

fn prepare(operation: &str, value: i32, ingredient: &str) -> String {
    operation.to_owned() + &" ".to_string() + &value.to_string() + &ingredient.to_owned()
}
fn preheat_oven(temp: i32, temp_circulation: i32) -> String{
    "Preheat the oven to ".to_string() + &temp.to_string() + &" °C ("+
    &temp_circulation.to_string() + &"°C convection)"
}
fn bake(time: i32) -> String{
    "Bake the casserole for ".to_string() + &time.to_string() + &"minutes"
}
```

COOKING FOR PROGRAMMERS 0x00

RICE VEGETABLE CASSEROLE
GO

```go
package main

import (
    "fmt"
    "time"
)

func main() {
    ingredients := map[string]string{
        "cheese":           "150g",
        "rice":             "250g",
        "oil":              "2 tbsp",
        "curry powder":     "2 tbsp",
        "vegetable broth": "500ml",
        "carrots":          "250g",
        "leeks or green onions": "to taste",
        "peas":             "200g",
        "eggs":             "2",
        "cream":            "250g",
        "cream cheese":     "50g",
    }
```

```go
instructions := []string{
    `Preheat the oven to 180°C.`,
    `Heat the oil in a pot and briefly stir-fry the rice in it.`,
    `Sprinkle curry powder over the rice and stir-fry briefly.`,
    `Pour the vegetable broth over the rice and bring to a boil,
    then simmer covered for about 10 minutes until the broth is
    absorbed by the rice.`,
    `Meanwhile, peel and dice the carrots, and slice the leeks
    or green onions finely.`,
    `Stir-fry the vegetables in the pan for about 5 minutes,
    then add the peas and season with salt and sugar to taste.`,
    `Mix the finished rice with the vegetable mixture and place
    in a casserole dish.`,
    `Beat the eggs in a bowl, add the cream and cream cheese,
    stir and season the sauce with salt and pepper.`,
    `Grate the cheese.`,
    `Spread the sauce over the rice and vegetable mixture and
    sprinkle with cheese.`,
    `Bake the casserole in the hot oven (middle) for 25 minutes.`,
}

fmt.Println("Ingredients:")
for ingredient, quantity := range ingredients {
    fmt.Printf("- %s: %s\n", ingredient, quantity)
}

fmt.Println("\nInstructions:")
for _, instruction := range instructions {
    fmt.Println(instruction)
}

time.Sleep(25 * time.Minute)

fmt.Println("\nThe casserole is now ready to serve.")
}
```

COOKING FOR PROGRAMMERS 0x00

CARROT CAKE
JAVA

```java
import java.util.Arrays;
import java.util.List;

public class CarrotCake {
    public static void main(String[] args) {
        List<RecipeStep> steps = Arrays.asList(
            new RecipeStep("Mix together", 3, "eggs", 250, "ml oil", 230, "g sugar"),
            new RecipeStep("Mix together", 200, "g flour", 2, "tsp baking powder", 2, "tsp cinnamon"),
            new RecipeStep("Combine", 0, "", 0, "", 0, ""),  // placeholder step
            new RecipeStep("Fold in", 100, "g walnuts", 300, "g carrots", 0, "")
        );
        preheatOven(180);
        for (int i = 0; i < steps.size(); i++) {
            RecipeStep step = steps.get(i);
            String mixture = step.prepare();
            System.out.println("Step " + (i + 1) + ": " + mixture);
        }
        bake("cake mixture", 45);
    }

    public static void preheatOven(int temperature) {
        System.out.println("Preheat the oven to " + temperature + "°C.");
    }

    public static void bake(String item, int minutes) {
        System.out.println("Bake the " + item + " for " + minutes + " minutes.");
    }
}
```

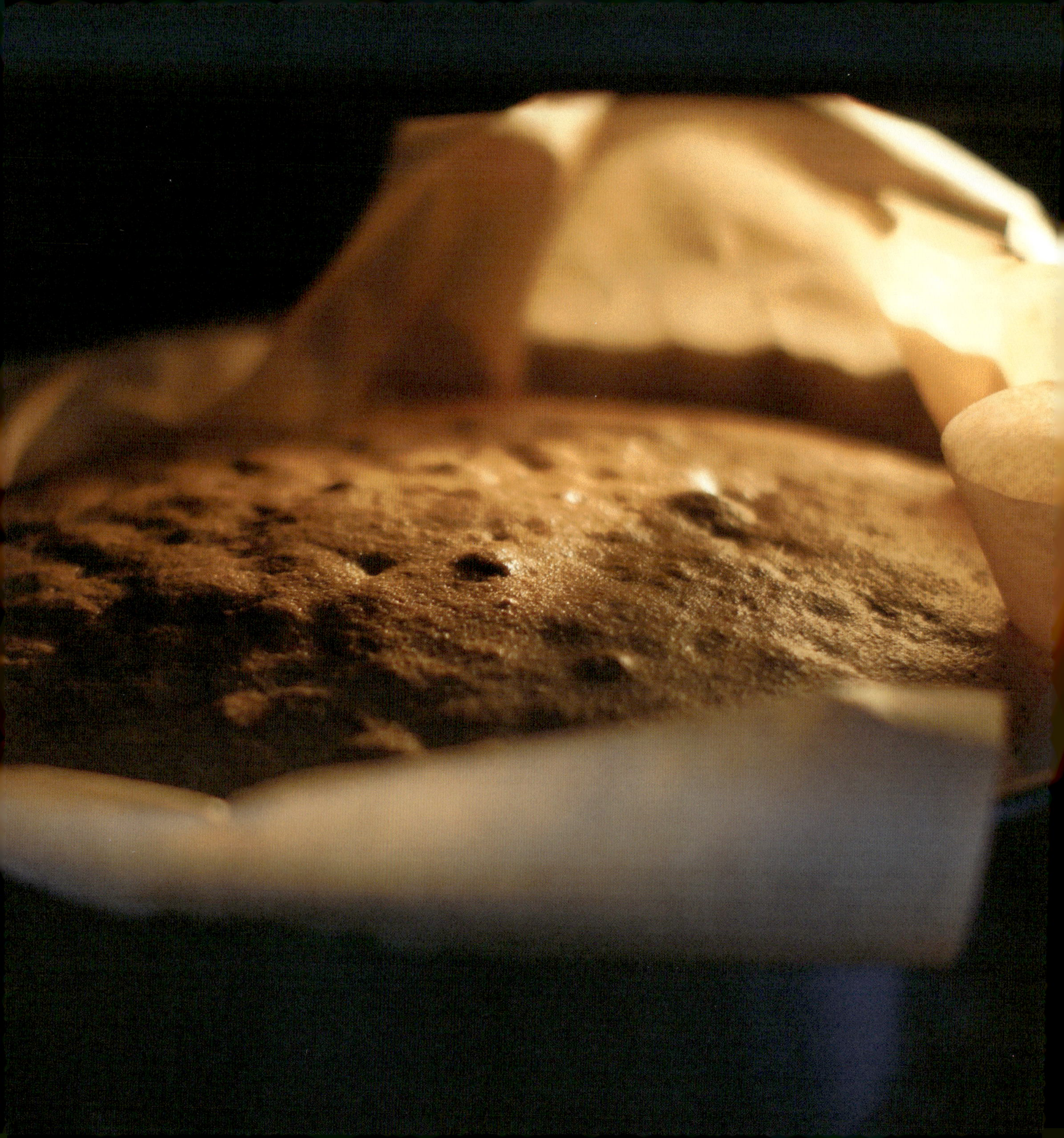

```java
class RecipeStep {
    private String operation;
    private int value1;
    private String ingredient1;
    private int value2;
    private String ingredient2;
    private int value3;
    private String ingredient3;

    public RecipeStep(String operation, int value1, String ingredient1,
    int value2, String ingredient2, int value3, String ingredient3) {
        this.operation = operation;
        this.value1 = value1;
        this.ingredient1 = ingredient1;
        this.value2 = value2;
        this.ingredient2 = ingredient2;
        this.value3 = value3;
        this.ingredient3 = ingredient3;
    }

    public String prepare() {
        return operation + " " + value1 + " " + ingredient1 + ", " + value2
        + " " + ingredient2 + ", and " + value3 + " " + ingredient3 + ".";
    }
}
```

SPICY MEAT STRUDEL
PERL

```perl
#!/usr/bin/perl
use strict;
use warnings;

my %recipe = (
    'name' => 'Spicy Meat Strudel',
    'description' => 'A puff pastry filled with a sautéed meat and
    vegetable mixture, layered with cream cheese, and baked until golden.',
    'ingredients' => [
        '500g minced meat',
        '1 onion',
        '2 tablespoons tomato paste',
        '1 to 2 tablespoons mustard',
        '1 leek',
        '1 to 2 bell peppers',
        '1 pack cream cheese',
        'Salt',
        'Pepper',
        'Hot paprika powder'
    ],
    'steps' => [
        'Sauté the minced meat and chopped onion. Season with salt,
        pepper, and hot paprika.',
        'Cut the bell peppers and leek, add to the pan, and sauté briefly.',
        'Add the tomato paste, mustard, and a little water. Stir well and let cool.',
        'Spread the mixture over a pre-made puff pastry.
        Spread cream cheese on top and shape into a strudel.',
        'Optionally, brush the strudel with an egg or some milk.',
        'Bake at 180°C (fan oven) for about 25 minutes.'
    ]
);
```

```perl
print "Recipe: $recipe{name}\n";
print "Description: $recipe{description}\n";
print "Ingredients:\n";
foreach my $ingredient (@{$recipe{ingredients}}) {
    print "- $ingredient\n";
}
print "Preparation steps:\n";
my $step_count = 1;
foreach my $step (@{$recipe{steps}}) {
    print "$step_count. $step\n";
    $step_count++;
}
```

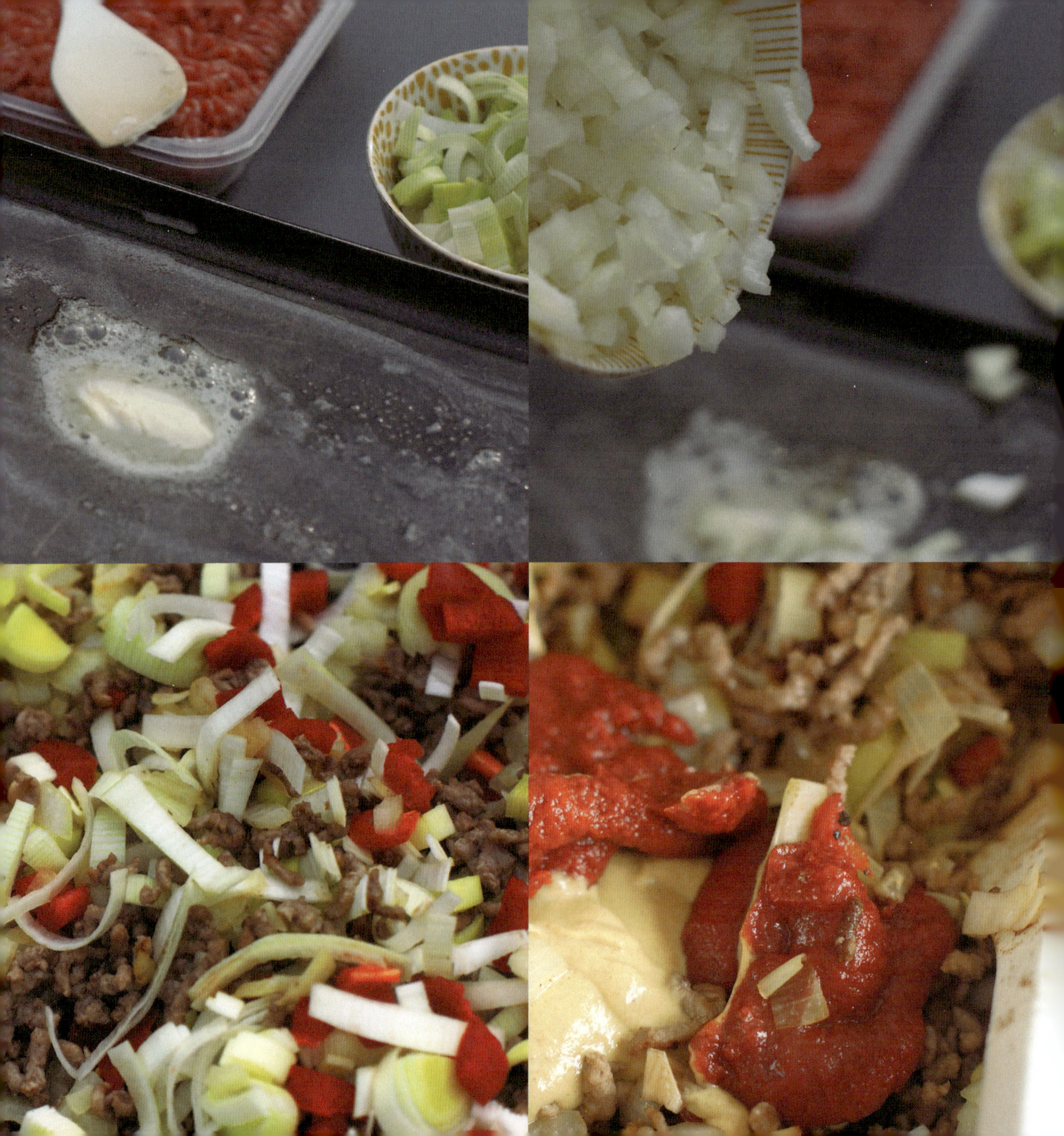

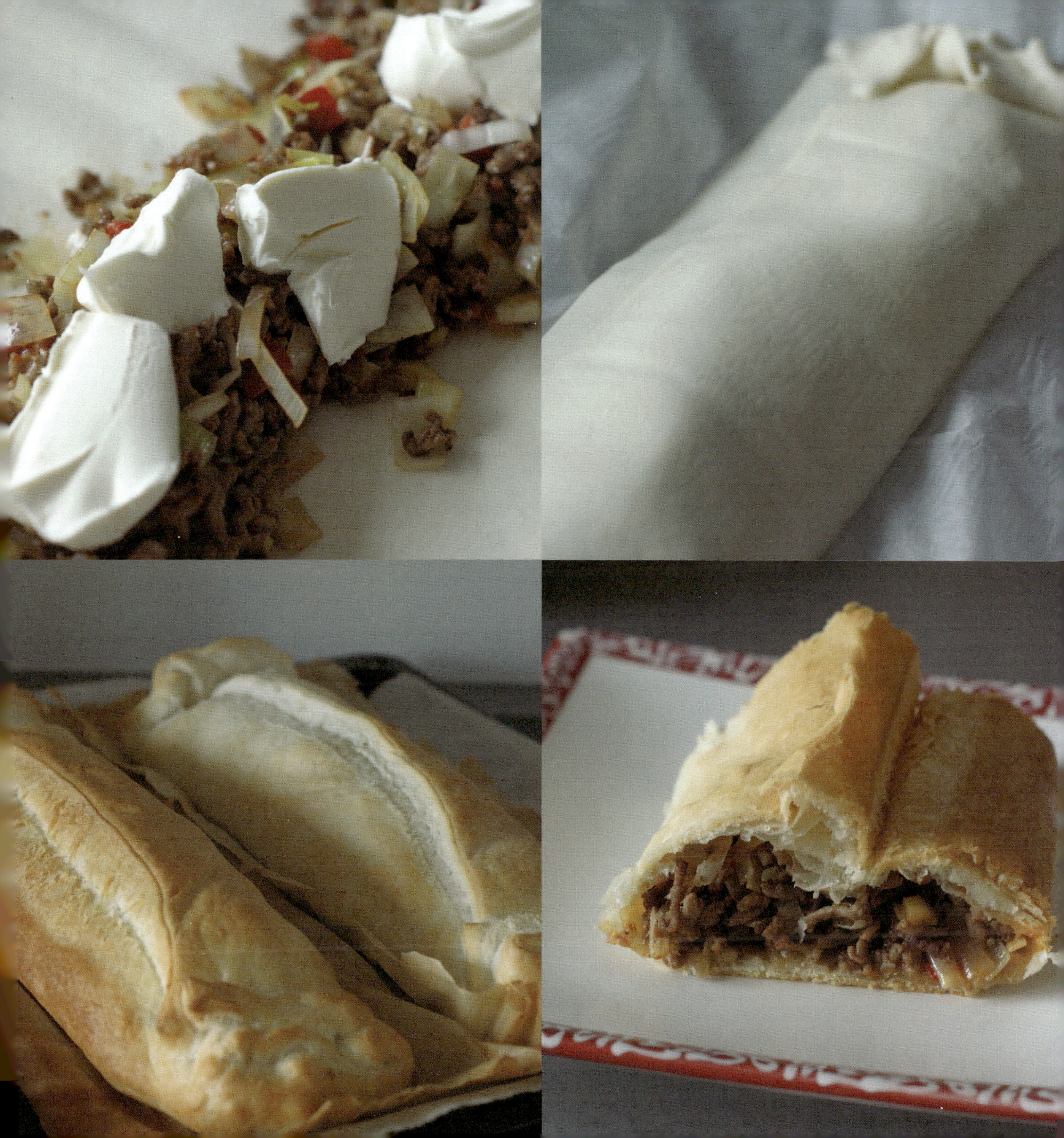

COOKING FOR PROGRAMMERS 0x00

EMPEROR'S MESS
SMALLTALK (GNU SMALLTALK)

```
Object subclass: Ingredient [
    Ingredient class >> name: aName amount: aAmount [
        ^self new
            name: aName;
            amount: aAmount;
            yourself
    ]

    | name amount |

    name: aName [ name := aName ]
    amount: aAmount [ amount := aAmount ]

    printOn: aStream [
        aStream
            nextPutAll: name;
            nextPutAll: ' : ';
            nextPutAll: amount asString
    ]
]
```

Wiener (Vienna) Kaiserschmarrn, often translated as "Emperor's Mess" or "Emperor's Shred", is a popular traditional dessert from Austria, also enjoyed in Bavaria, Germany. It's a type of shredded, caramelized pancake that is made with a sweet, egg-based batter, and often includes a variety of mix-ins such as raisins, nuts, or apples.

COOKING FOR PROGRAMMERS 0x00

```
Object subclass: Kaiserschmarrn [
    | ingredients steps |

    Kaiserschmarrn class >> new [
        ^super new
            initializeIngredients;
            initializeSteps;
            yourself
    ]

    initializeIngredients [ ingredients := OrderedCollection new ]
    initializeSteps [ steps := OrderedCollection new ]

    addIngredient: aName withAmount: aNumber [
        ingredients add: (Ingredient name: aName amount: aNumber)
    ]

    addStep: aString [
        steps add: aString
    ]

    printOn: aStream [
        aStream nextPutAll: 'Ingredients:'; cr.
        ingredients do: [ :each |
            aStream print: each; cr
        ].
        aStream nextPutAll: 'Steps:'; cr.
        steps do: [ :each |
            aStream nextPutAll: each; cr
        ]
    ]
]
```

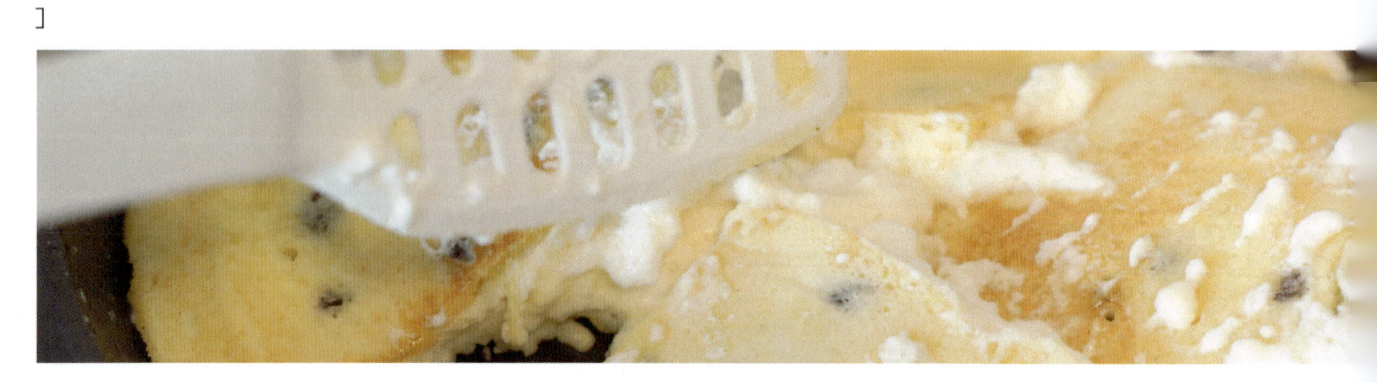

COOKING FOR PROGRAMMERS 0x00

```smalltalk
| recipe |
recipe := Kaiserschmarrn new.
recipe addIngredient: 'Flour' withAmount: 200.
recipe addIngredient: 'Sugar' withAmount: 35.
recipe addIngredient: 'Eggs' withAmount: 4.
recipe addIngredient: 'Milk' withAmount: (3 / 10).
recipe addIngredient: 'Butter' withAmount: 'a bit'.
recipe addIngredient: 'Raisins' withAmount: 'to taste'.
recipe addIngredient: 'Icing sugar' withAmount: 'for dusting'.
recipe addStep: 'Separate the eggs.'.
recipe addStep: 'Whip the egg whites to stiff peaks.'.
recipe addStep: 'Mix flour, sugar, yolks and milk to a smooth, thick dough.'.
recipe addStep: 'Fold the whipped egg whites into the dough.'.
recipe addStep: 'Add raisins to the mixture.'.
recipe addStep: 'Melt butter in a large pan.'.
recipe addStep: 'Slowly bake the dough on both sides.'.
recipe addStep: 'Tear the dough into pieces and continue baking for a short time.'.
recipe addStep: 'Serve Kaiserschmarrn on plates, dust with sugar and serve with compote or applesauce (as shown with pineapple pieces).'.
Transcript show: (recipe printString); cr.
```

COOKING FOR PROGRAMMERS 0x00

CREAMY HAM SPÄTZLE
HASKELL

```haskell
module Main where

data Ingredient = Ingredient String String
data Step = Step String

data Recipe = Recipe
  { title :: String
  , ingredients :: [Ingredient]
  , steps :: [Step]
  }

instance Show Ingredient where
   show (Ingredient name quantity) = quantity ++ " of " ++ name

instance Show Step where
   show (Step description) = description

printRecipe :: Recipe -> IO ()
printRecipe recipe = do
  putStrLn $ "Recipe: " ++ (title recipe)
  putStrLn "\nIngredients:"
  mapM_ (putStrLn . show) (ingredients recipe)
  putStrLn "\nSteps:"
  mapM_ (putStrLn . show) (steps recipe)
```

```haskell
main :: IO ()
main = do
  let ingredients = [ Ingredient "Ham (0.5cm thick)" "150g"
                    , Ingredient "Sour cream" "250g"
                    , Ingredient "Broccoli" "to taste"
                    , Ingredient "Onion" "1"
                    , Ingredient "Ready-made or homemade egg spaetzle" ""
                    , Ingredient "Soup broth" "1/8l"
                    ]
  let steps = [ Step "Roast the onion in a pan."
              , Step "Add the spaetzle and fry it with the onions."
              , Step "Deglaze with the soup broth."
              , Step "Dice the ham and fry it in the pan."
              , Step "Reduce the heat, then stir in the sour cream."
              , Step "Season with salt and pepper to taste."
              , Step "Stir in the cooked broccoli."
              , Step "Serve and enjoy your creamy ham spaetzle."
              ]
  let recipe = Recipe "Creamy Ham Spaetzle" ingredients steps
  printRecipe recipe
```

SOUTH TYROLEAN APPLE STRUDEL
ADA (ADA 2012)

```ada
with Ada.Text_IO; use Ada.Text_IO;
with Ada.Strings.Unbounded; use Ada.Strings.Unbounded;
with Ada.Containers.Vectors;

procedure Print_Recipe is
   type Unit is (Grams, Teaspoons, Packs, Pieces, None);

   type Amount is record
      Quantity : Natural;
      U : Unit;
   end record;

   type Ingredient is record
      Name : Unbounded_String;
      A : Amount;
   end record;

   type Step is record
      Description : Unbounded_String;
   end record;

   package Ingredient_Vectors is new
   Ada.Containers.Vectors (Index_Type => Natural, Element_Type => Ingredient);
   package Step_Vectors is new Ada.Containers.Vectors (Index_Type => Natural, Element_Type => Step);

   Ingredients : Ingredient_Vectors.Vector;
   Steps : Step_Vectors.Vector;

   Temp_Ingredient : Ingredient;
   Temp_Step : Step;

begin
   Ingredients.Append ((Name => To_Unbounded_String(
    "ready-made shortcrust pastry from the supermarket or homemade shortcrust pastry"
    ),A => (Quantity => 2, U => Packs)));
   Ingredients.Append ((Name => To_Unbounded_String("apples"), A => (Quantity => 800, U => Grams)));
   Ingredients.Append ((Name => To_Unbounded_String("sugar"), A => (Quantity => 60, U => Grams)));
   Ingredients.Append ((Name => To_Unbounded_String("vanilla sugar"), A => (Quantity => 2, U => Packs)));
   Ingredients.Append ((Name => To_Unbounded_String(
    "breadcrumbs (dried bread crumbs)"), A => (Quantity => 80, U => Grams)));
```

```ada
Ingredients.Append ((Name => To_Unbounded_String("raisins"), A => (Quantity => 60, U => Grams)));
Ingredients.Append ((Name => To_Unbounded_String("pine nuts"), A => (Quantity => 40, U => Grams)));
Ingredients.Append ((Name => To_Unbounded_String("cinnamon"), A => (Quantity => 1, U => Teaspoons)));
Ingredients.Append ((Name => To_Unbounded_String(
"egg or a splash of milk for brushing the dough"), A => (Quantity => 1, U => None)));

Steps.Append ((Description => To_Unbounded_String("Peel and thinly slice the apples.")));
Steps.Append ((Description => To_Unbounded_String("Roughly chop the pine nuts.")));
Steps.Append ((Description => To_Unbounded_String(
"In a bowl, thoroughly mix the apples, sugar, breadcrumbs, raisins, pine nuts, and cinnamon.")));
Steps.Append ((Description => To_Unbounded_String(
"Fill the long shortcrust pastry with the mixture.")));
Steps.Append ((Description => To_Unbounded_String(
"Bake at 190 degrees Celsius (top/bottom heat) for 45 minutes in the oven.")));
Put_Line ("Recipe: South Tyrolean Shortcrust Apple Strudel");
Put_Line ("Ingredients:");
for Ing of Ingredients loop
   Put (Item => Ing.A.Quantity'Image);
   case Ing.A.U is
      when Grams => Put_Line ("g " & To_String(Ing.Name));
      when Teaspoons => Put_Line (" tsp " & To_String(Ing.Name));
      when Packs => Put_Line (" pack(s) " & To_String(Ing.Name));
      when Pieces => Put_Line (" piece(s) " & To_String(Ing.Name));
      when None => Put_Line (To_String(Ing.Name));
   end case;
end loop;

Put_Line ("Instructions:");
for St of Steps loop
   Put_Line (To_String(St.Description));
end loop;

end Print_Recipe;
```

Ada

In Strong Typing We Trust

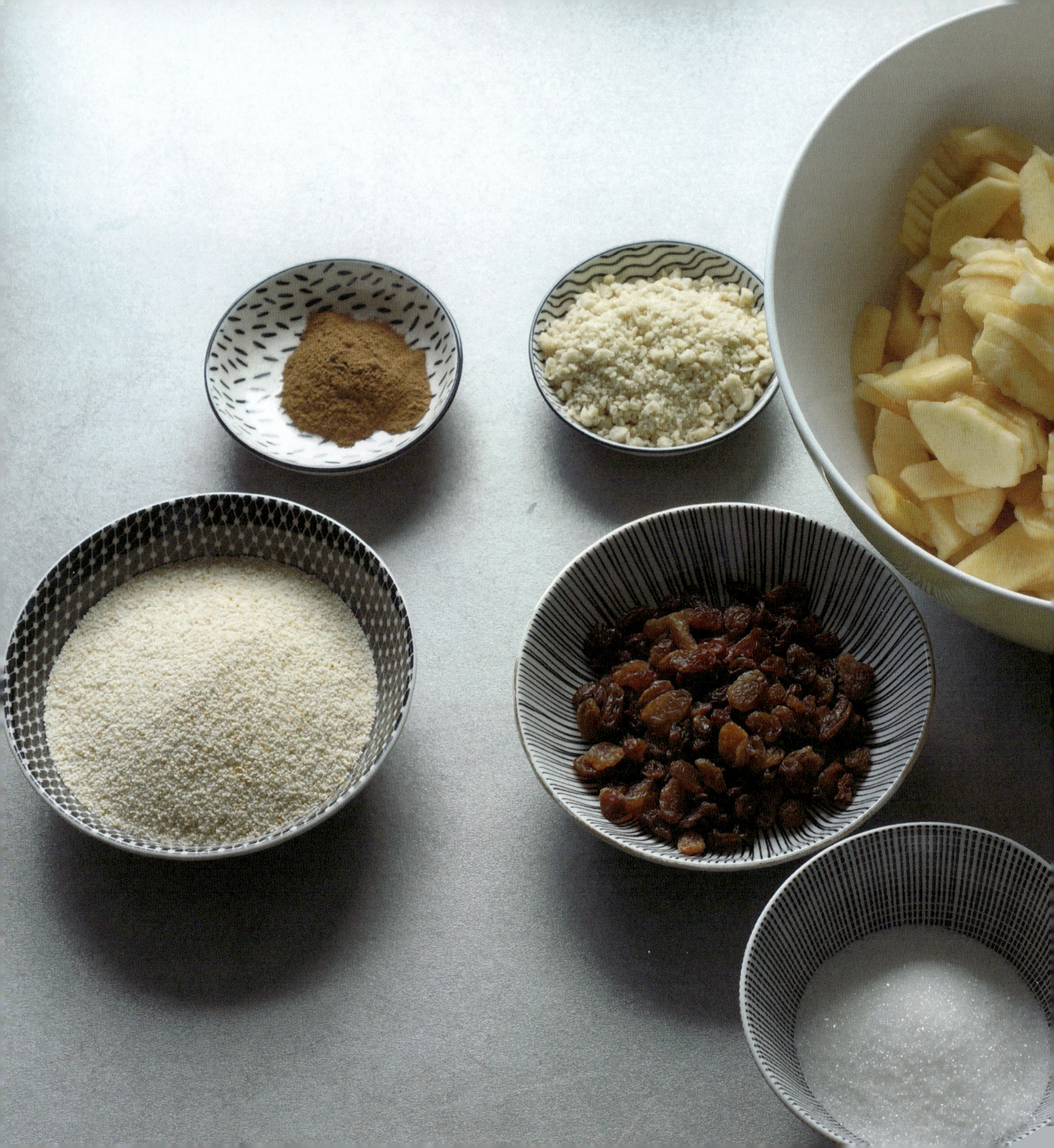

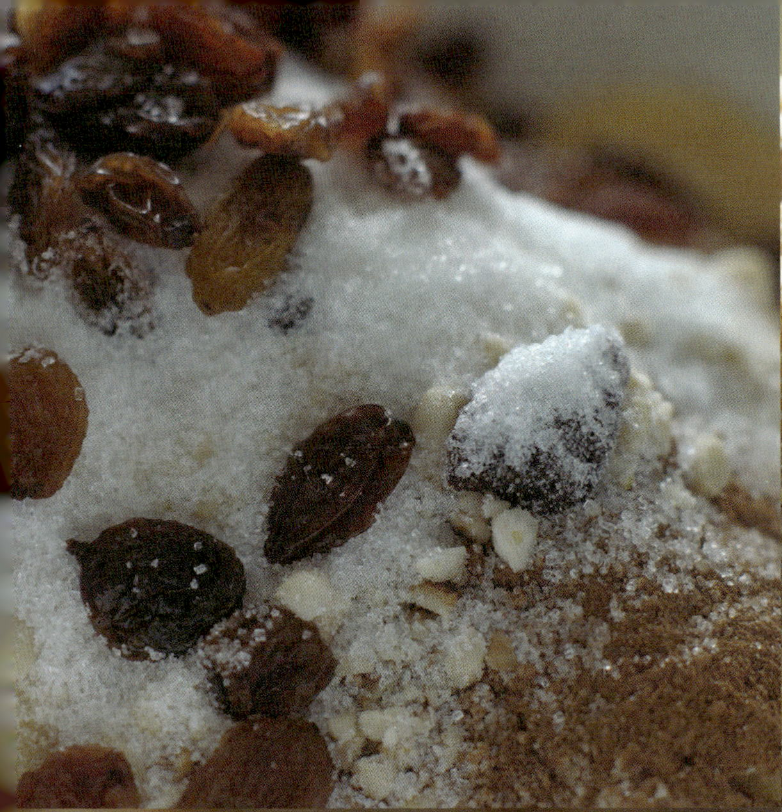
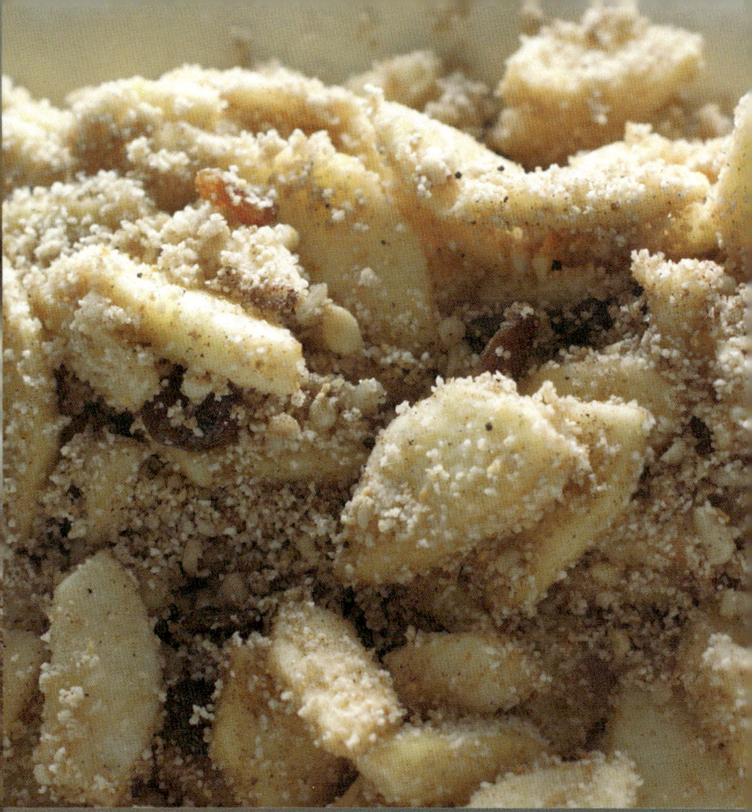
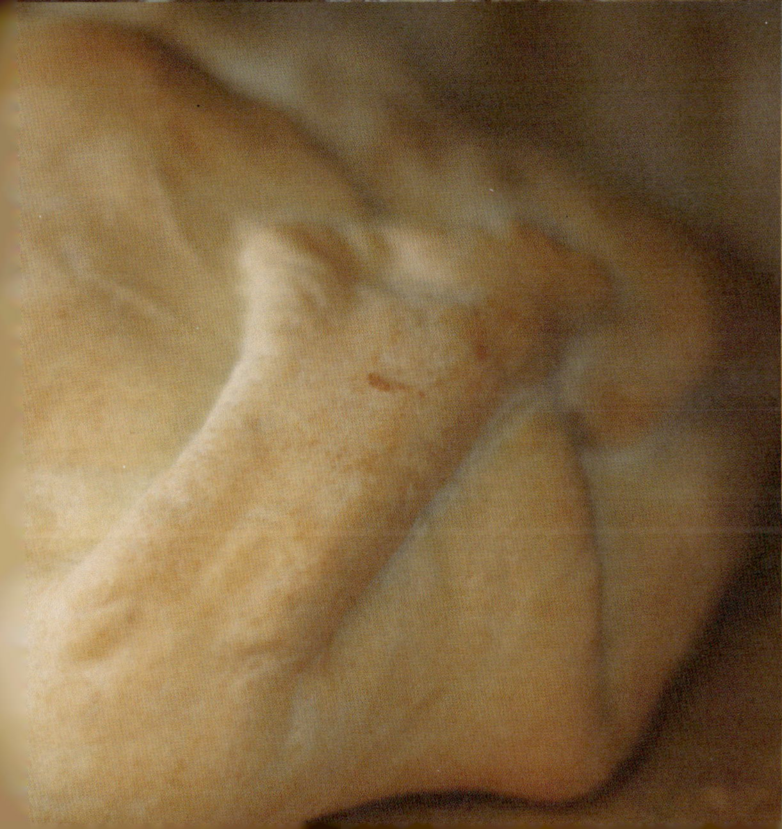
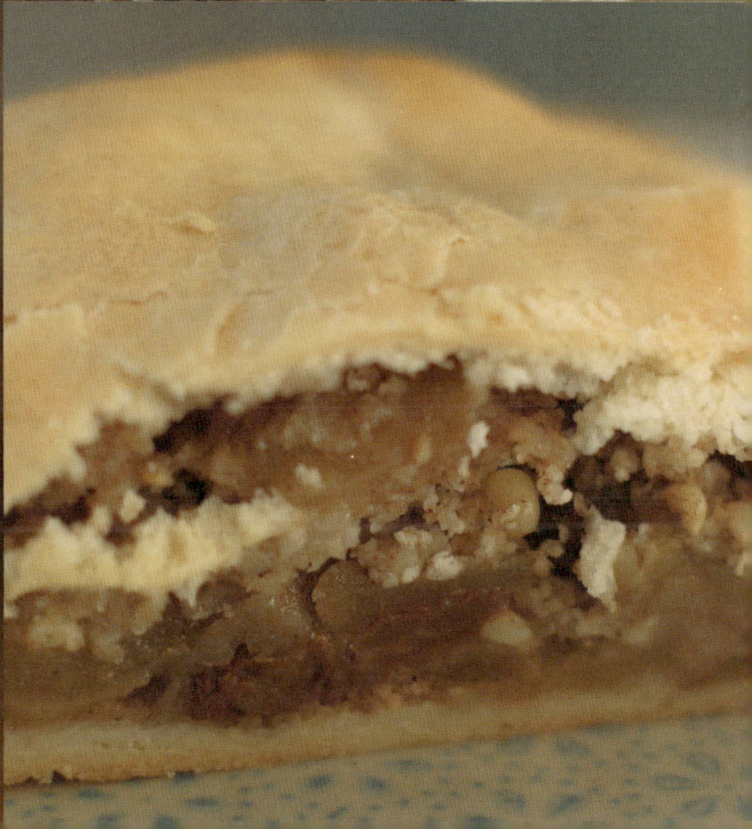

???
BRAINFUCK

```
+[--------->++<]>+.----.---------
.-[--->+<]>---.[---->+<]>+++.[->+
++<]>++.+++++++++++++.------.+++.
--------.-.-[--->+<]>-.+[->+++<]>+
+.++..+[->+++<]>++.[-->+<]>+++.[-
->+++++++<]>.--------.----.+++++++
++++++.++++[->+++<]>+.++.--[--->+
<]>-.+[->+++<]>++.++..---[->+++<]
>.-------------.+[->+++<]>.++++++++
+++++..-----.-[++>---<]>+.------[->
++<]>-.--[--->++<]>--.+[----->+<]
>.----.+++++.+++++++.-.+++[->+++<
]>.[--->+<]>----.+[---->+<]>+++.-
[--->++<]>-.+++++.-[->+++++<]>-.[
->+++<]>++.+++++++++++++.------.+
++.---.+++++.--------.-[--->+<]>--
.--[->++++<]>-.-[->+++<]>-.--[---
>+<]>-.+++[->+++<]>.++++++++++++++.
```

— 42 —

NOTES

The notes page is a place for you to write down any personal modifications or additional information about recipes, such as ingredient substitutions or cooking times.

ATTRIBUTION/COPYRIGHT NOTICES

"The R logo" by The R Foundation is licensed under Creative Commons Attribution-ShareAlike 4.0 International (Source: https://www.r-project.org/logo/): https://creativecommons.org/licenses/by-sa/4.0/

"The Ruby logo" by Yukihiro Matsumoto is licensed under Creative Commons Attribution-ShareAlike 2.5 (Source: https://www.ruby-lang.org/en/about/logo/): https://creativecommons.org/licenses/by-sa/2.5/

"The Rust logo" by The Rust Foundation is licensed under Creative Commons Attribution 4.0 International (Source: https://foundation.rust-lang.org/policies/logo-policy-and-media-guide/): https://creativecommons.org/licenses/by/4.0/

"The PHP logo" by Colin Viebrock is licensed under Creative Commons Attribution-ShareAlike 4.0 International (Source: https://www.php.net/download-logos.php): https://creativecommons.org/licenses/by-sa/4.0/

"The Typescript logo" by Microsoft is licensed under the Apache License, Version 2.0 (the "License"); http://www.apache.org/licenses/LICENSE-2.0

"The C++ logo" is a trademark of the Standard C++ Foundation (https://isocpp.org/about), Terms: https://isocpp.org/home/terms-of-use

MATLAB is a registered trademark of The MathWorks,Inc., USA; info@mathworks.com

"The GO logo" by Google Inc. is licensed under Creative Commons Attribution 4.0 International (Source: https://go.dev/copyright): https://creativecommons.org/licenses/by/4.0/

"The Perl Raptor logo" by Sebastian Riedel is licensed under Creative Commons Attribution-ShareAlike 3.0 Unported (CC BY-SA 3.0) (Source: https://github.com/pfig/perl-raptor): https://creativecommons.org/licenses/by-sa/3.0/

"The GNU Smalltalk logo" by Mike Anderson is licensed under Creative Commons Attribution-ShareAlike 3.0 Unported (CC BY-SA 3.0): https://creativecommons.org/licenses/by-sa/3.0/

"The Haskell logo" is licensed under the simple permissive license: https://wiki.haskell.org/HaskellWiki:Licensing

"Java" is a registered trademarks of Oracle and/or its affiliates

COOKING FOR PROGRAMMERS 0x00

by Richard Wurzer

Richard Wurzer Electrical Engineering
Hain 45
3644 Emmersdorf
Austria

https://www.rwurzer.com/cooking
office@rwurzer.com

Copyright 2023 Richard Wurzer.

07-2023: Second Edition

All rights reserved. No part of this publication may be reproduced, distributed, or transmitted in any form or by any means, including photocopying, recording, or other electronic or mechanical methods, without the prior written permission of the publisher, except in the case of brief quotations embodied in critical reviews and certain other noncommercial uses permitted by copyright law.

Cover design by Richard Wurzer.

Richard Wurzer Electrical Engineering is not affiliated with Amazon.com, Inc. or its affiliates.

This book was published using Amazon KDP (Kindle Direct Publishing).

ISBN: 9798371374615

INDEX

A
Ada - 38, 39
Apples - 38
Apple Strudel - 38, 39

B
Basil - 22
Beans - 12, 13
Brainfuck - 42
Bread crumbs - 38
Broccoli - 37
Butter - 18, 19, 22, 35

C
Cake - 18, 19, 25, 32
Carbonara - 10, 11
Casserole - 24
Carrotcake - 25
Carrots - 16, 23, 24, 25
Carrot Cake - 25, 27
Cheese - 6, 16, 18, 19, 22, 23, 24, 28
Cheesecake - 18, 19, 30
Cherry - 4
Chocolate - 9
Cinnamon - 9, 25, 39
Coconut - 14, 15
Coffee - 12, 13
Cream - 6, 22, 23, 24, 28
Crepes - 17
Curd Cake - 18, 19
Curry - 23, 24
C++ - 6
C# - 18

E
Eggs - 17, 19, 23, 24, 25, 35
Emperor's Mess - 32, 34, 35
Espresso - 12, 13

F
Feta - 16
Flour - 10, 25, 35

G
Garlic - 4, 5, 10
GO - 23, 24

H
Ham - 12, 36, 37
Ham Spätzle - 36, 37
Haskell - 36, 37
Herbs - 4, 5, 14

I
Icing sugar - 35

J
Java - 25, 27
Javascript - 4, 5
Juice - 14

L
Leek - 28
Lemon - 14

M
Marjoram - 4

Matlab® - 16
Meat Strudel - 28, 29
Milk - 9, 10, 14, 17, 28, 35, 39
Millet - 16
Millet with Vegatables - 16
Minced meat - 28
Mozzarella - 22
Mushrooms - 4, 5
Mustard - 28

N
Noodles - 10
Nuts - 9, 25, 32, 39

O
Olive - 4
Onions - 6, 16, 23, 24, 28, 37
Oregano - 4
Oven Vegetables - 4

P
Palatschinken - 17
Paprika - 5, 28,
Parmesan - 22
Parsley - 10
Pasta - 10
Peas - 23, 24
Pepper - 4, 5, 6, 10, 14, 20, 22, 28
Peppers - 4, 5, 16
Perl - 28
PHP - 8
Pine nuts - 39
Pizza - 6
Pizza toast - 6

Potatoes - 4, 5
Pudding - 9
Python - 12, 13

R
R - 22
Raisins - 35
Rice - 9, 23, 24
Rice Pudding - 8
Rice Vegetable Casserole - 23, 24
Risotto - 9
Rosemary - 4
Ruby - 17

S
Salt - 5, 6, 9, 10, 14, 22, 24, 28, 37
Shallots - 4, 5
Simple Carbonara - 10, 11
Smalltalk - 32, 34, 35
Soup - 14, 15, 37
Sour cream - 37
Spaghetti - 10
Spices - 9, 14, 16
Sugar - 9, 14, 17, 19, 24, 25, 35, 38, 39

T
Toast - 6
Tomato Coconut Soup - 14, 15
Tomato paste - 28
Turkey - 22
Turkey in the Oven - 22
Typescript - 10, 11

V
Vanilla - 9, 38
Vegetables - 4, 5, 16, 24

W
Walnuts - 25

Printed in Great Britain
by Amazon